IRELAND

Recipes, Flavors & Traditions

P.J. Tierney

KITCHEN INK's passionate Kids in the Kitchen team of recipe creators, testers, editors, food stylists, photographers, and designers work tirelessly to create products that introduce kids to cooking. Having fun, making memories in the kitchen, and creating a delicious meal is what we are all about.

Our easy-to-follow, creative, and delicious recipes—kid-tested and parent-approved—include both healthy meals and special treats. Adult supervision and safety first are always important in the kitchen. We hope you enjoy our books as much as we have loved creating them.

Download a free culinary passport pdf. This passport has all pages; it does not contain the stickers found in the culinary passport sold with *The Global Cookbook, Delicious Recipes from Seven Continents.*
ISBN: 978-1-943016-22-8
www.kitcheninkpublishing.com

Recipes, text, and photographs by Kitchen Ink Publishing.

Publisher's Note
While every care has been taken in compiling the recipes for this book, neither Kitchen Ink Publishing, nor any other persons who have worked on this publication, can accept responsibility for any errors or omissions, inadvertent or not, that may be found in the recipes or text, nor for any problems that may arise as a result of preparing these recipes. If you have any special dietary requirements, restrictions, or medical conditions, it is advisable to consult a medical professional before following any of the recipes contained in this book.

Library of Congress Cataloging-in-Publication data is available.
ISBN 978-1-943016-29-7

First Edition
29 28 27 26 10 9 8 7 6 5 4 3 2 1

Printed in China

Kitchen Ink Publishing
114 John Street, #277
New York, NY 10038

Kitchen Ink books may be purchased for educational, business, or sales promotional use. For information, please email the Special Markets Department at sales@kitcheninkpublishing.com.

See what Kitchen Ink is up to, share recipes and tips, and shop our store—www.kitcheninkpublishing.com.

kitcheninkpublishing

For my big brother,
our Nolan namesake,
William Patrick Nolan
Bill, I am so lucky to have you in my life and it's wonderful watching you share our family traditions with the next generation. Love ya!

Introduction by P.J. Tierney

This cookbook honors my family's Irish traditions. All four of my grandparents emigrated to New York from Ireland, so this is a tribute to the Mollys and Tarpeys from County Mayo and to the Sullivans and Nolans from County Kerry.

I first visited Ireland when I was 12 with my grandmother and Aunt Patsy. I was a picky eater and for the entire trip, I survived on nothing but brown bread and butter. Making this bread recipe on page 2 transports me back to Ireland, although both my tastes and Ireland's culinary landscape, thankfully, have evolved. Yes, there are a lot of meat and potato recipes, but now many gastropubs and restaurants offer vegetarian options.

I am excited to share this collection of recipes including traditional Irish recipes, adopted recipes you will find all over Ireland, and my addition of kid-friendly, fun recipes—for example, the leprechaun cake hat recipe on page 74, which reveals the surprise rainbow when cut.

Growing up, I spent my summers in the Catskill Mountains of New York. On the last day of school, we would pack the car and drive 2 ½ hours north of NYC to the town of East Durham, New York, nicknamed "The Emerald Isle of the Catskills."

In the 1950s, my mother's family opened and ran Tarpey's Palm Inn, a family resort with hotel rooms, bungalows, and a bar and restaurant. There were lots of activities, including swimming in the creek or the in-ground pool, handball courts, ball games, horseback riding, live entertainment, and a dance hall. Three meals a day were served in a formal dining room; Irish soda bread was a staple. I share my grandmother's recipe on page 6. East Durham became a popular destination for the New York and Boston Irish with its family-friendly resorts with live Irish music, talent shows, and Irish step dancing. Yes, at one point there were shamrocks painted on the road.

By time I was born, Tarpey's was no longer in operation, but many Irish resorts including The Shamrock House, Gavin's Golden Hill, McGrath's Edgewood Falls, and The Blackthorne are still in operation today. One can stop into the Guaranteed Irish shop for all things Ireland. Each Memorial Day weekend, thousands flock to East Durham for the Irish Festival, a three-day event celebrating Irish traditions, Irish music, folklore, and food. Book your stay now as the resorts and campgrounds in and around East Durham sell out (my plug for this town that will always have my heart).

Did you know? Corned Beef and Cabbage (see page 56) is not popular in Ireland; this meal was created by Irish Americans and is now a staple of St. Patrick's Day celebrations.

Potatoes are often included with every meal. You will find a quintessential mashed potato recipe on page 32 which is the foundation for Boxty (page 9), Colcannon (page 30), and the topping of Shepherd's Pie. This main dish is traditionally made with lamb and is named after the shepherds who would tend their flocks. Today, lamb is often replaced with beef for this beloved recipe. I like this recipe so much that I included three options: page 49 for the traditional way made with ground lamb or beef, mini shepherd's pies perfect for a party (page 34), and if you prefer a vegetarian option, see page 64 for one made with lentils and vegetables. I encourage you to add or replace ingredients and make each recipe in this book your own.

Turn to page 52 for bangers and mash. "Bangers" is slang for sausages, a term that originated during World War I when sausages were made with high water content and fillers, causing them to "bang" or explode when cooked. "Mash" simply refers to the mashed potatoes served with the sausages.

Seafood also plays a main role in Ireland's cuisine; fish was traditionally eaten on Fridays in homes throughout Ireland. You will find a delicious seafood pie recipe on page 46, Fish Cakes page 37, and roasted salmon on page 54. In every town you will find a fish & chips shop; turn to page 60 for this delicious recipe and discover that "chips" are fries.

Tea at any time of day is perfectly paired with fruit scones (page 16) made with cranberries or raisins, tea cake (page 80), and lace (page 84) or shortbread (page 71) cookies.

Tea Brack (page 18) is a thick bread made with tea-soaked raisins and dates. A tradition I discovered is that during Christmas, people bake symbolic objects into this fruitcake, such as a ring for marriage within the year, a piece of cloth for bad luck, or a coin for wealth. I was happy to learn that the ring is the most popular and the cloth not so much.

This book is part of the Culinary Passport Series; when you complete Wicklow Pancakes, page 4, Corned Beef and Cabbage, page 56, and the Leprechaun Hat Rainbow Cake, page 74, place the corresponding sticker in your culinary passport or mark the recipe to track your success and journey around the world through food.

Wild blackberries grow commonly on bushes in Ireland along country roads, hedgerows, and in parks. Picking them from late July through September has been a traditional, seasonal activity for generations. The fruit grows on bramble bushes, which are a native plant in Ireland and an important part of the country's biodiversity. Pick up some berries and make the Blackberry Sorbet recipe on page 78.

I explore Irish Folklore on page 91, the foundation of many Irish traditions. Learn about fairies and kissing the Blarney Stone.

Preparing all the recipes in a book is challenging and will take time. You may want to pass on a recipe you think you may not like, You don't have to like every recipe, but make and taste it – you might be surprised. Once you complete all the recipes in the book, congratulations! Cross off the Ireland book in your Culinary Passport. Quite the accomplishment!

Thanks for joining me on this culinary adventure.

P.J. Tierney

A Note from the Kids in the Kitchen Team

Each recipe notes the number of servings and the time needed to prepare the dish. Please note, the recommended chilling time for a dish may not be included in its active preparation time.

This cookbook includes easy recipes and those requiring a little more patience and skill. As you become more comfortable preparing recipes, it is important to be challenged and improve your kitchen skills.

An adult should be with you to assist, especially when using a knife and the stovetop, and when putting your delicious dishes into and bringing them out of the hot oven. It is up to the adult to decide when you can be more independent in the kitchen.

Step-by-step directions tell you what you need to prepare the dish. Read each recipe completely before you begin and make sure you have all the tools and ingredients you need. These recipes are written for kids all around the globe and both US measurements and metrics are included.

Sometimes a recipe may call for an ingredient you do not have. A substitution will be offered for an international ingredient that may be challenging to find. Please note that if an ingredient is marked "optional," you can leave it out of the recipe if you choose.

If you are vegetarian, you will find recipes without meat or with suggestions to prepare meatless versions of the dish.

Everyone is excited to taste the food they have created BUT, hit the brakes. Food is piping hot when removed from the oven. Always be patient and let the food cool before sampling. Your tongue will thank you.

Always clean up the kitchen when you are done and remember that more hands make light work. Have a cleanup party and everyone is rewarded with dessert.

Contents

Breakfast

Small Plates, Sides & Snacks

Entrées

Desserts

Breakfast

Brown Bread

 1 hour 40 minutes

 1 loaf

Ingredients

2 cups (226 grams) whole wheat flour

2 cups (226 grams) all-purpose flour

4 ½ tablespoons (56 grams) granulated sugar

2 teaspoons (10 milliliters) baking powder

1 teaspoon (5 grams) baking soda

1 ½ teaspoons (10 grams) salt

½ cup (43 grams) Irish rolled oats—do not use quick oats

1 ¾ cups (415 milliliters) buttermilk

TIP

Let the bread rest for 30 minutes before slicing. The moisture in the bread needs time to disperse; if you slice it too soon, the middle of the loaf will be gummy.

Directions

1. Preheat oven to 450°F (230°C).
2. In a large bowl, mix the whole wheat flour, all-purpose flour, sugar, baking powder, baking soda, salt, and oats.
3. Pour in most of the buttermilk and stir it into the dry ingredients. If the mixture still seems very dry, stir in the rest of the buttermilk.
4. With floured hands, knead into a ball. Shape the dough into a circle and place on a lined baking sheet. Press flat to about 2 inches (5 centimeters) thick. It will form a round loaf about 8 inches (20 centimeters) in diameter.
5. With a sharp knife, cut a deep cross on the top of the ball.
6. Bake in the preheated oven for 15 minutes. Reduce the heat to 400°F (200°C) then bake for an additional 25 to 30 minutes. The bread should be risen and browned, and sound hollow when tapped on the bottom.

Wicklow Pancakes

25 minutes

2 servings

Ingredients

1 tablespoon (15 milliliters) butter

2 eggs, large

1 cup (240 milliliters) milk

1 cup (60 grams) plain breadcrumbs

2 teaspoons (6 grams) fresh parsley, chopped

1 teaspoon (1 gram) fresh chives, chopped

1 teaspoon (1 gram) fresh thyme leaves

¼ teaspoon salt (1.5 grams)

¼ teaspoon pepper (1 gram)

Additional herbs for garnish (optional)

Directions

1. In a large skillet over medium-low heat, melt half the butter.
2. In a large bowl, crack the eggs and whisk until smooth. Stir in the milk, breadcrumbs, parsley, chives and thyme. Season with salt and pepper.
3. When the butter is hot, pour the egg/breadcrumb mixture into the pan, evening out to cover the bottom. Continue to cook over medium-low to low heat until eggs begin to set and bottom is lightly browned, about 6 minutes. Carefully flip the pancake and cook on the other side until firm and browned, another 5 or 6 minutes.
4. Cut in quarters and top each with a dab of remaining butter. Garnish with additional fresh herbs, if you like.

Soda Bread

55 minutes

1 loaf

Ingredients

4 cups (452 grams) all-purpose flour

1 teaspoon (6 grams) baking soda

1 teaspoon (6 grams) salt

1 tablespoon (12.5 grams) granulated sugar

2 cups (480 milliliters) buttermilk

1 cup (155 grams) raisins or currants, optional

1 ½ teaspoon (3 grams) caraway seeds, optional

Directions

1. Preheat the oven to 450°F (230°C). Line a large baking sheet with parchment paper and set aside.
2. In a large mixing bowl, sift together the flour, soda, salt, and sugar. Whisk together until well combined.
3. Make a well in the center of the dry ingredients; pour in the buttermilk. Mix together using a rubber spatula for about 30 seconds, until the mixture forms a loose dough. Don't overwork the dough – overmixing can make the interior rubbery. Add the raisins and caraway seeds (if using) and mix in quickly, about 10 seconds more.

4. Turn the dough out onto a lightly floured work surface. Knead briefly until the dough sticks together, about 3 to 4 turns. Form the dough into a ball. Transfer the dough to the prepared baking sheet.
5. Carefully score a cross in the top of the loaf using a large, serrated knife to a depth of about 1 inch (2.5 centimeters). Immediately transfer it to the preheated oven.
6. Bake for 40 to 45 minutes, or until the bread is split at the cross and the crust is well browned. The loaf should be well risen and sound hollow when tapped on the bottom with your knuckles.
7. Let bread cool slightly before slicing; serve warm.

Boxty (Irish Potato Pancakes) with Sour Cream and Chive Sauce

30 minutes

6 servings

Ingredients

TIP
Leftover mashed potatoes are perfect for this recipe.

Pancakes

2 cups (420 grams) cold mashed potatoes

2 cups (300 grams) grated raw russet potatoes

2 cups (240 grams) all-purpose flour

1 ½ teaspoons (9 grams) salt

1 teaspoon (5 grams) baking soda

1 ½ to 2 cups (360 to 480 milliliters) buttermilk, plus more as needed

2 tablespoons (30 milliliters) butter for frying

Optional add-ins: Chopped green onions/scallions, shredded white cheddar cheese

Sour Cream and Chive Sauce

1 cup (240 grams) sour cream

¼ teaspoon (0.8 grams) onion powder

¼ teaspoon (1.4 grams) garlic powder

¼ teaspoon (0.7 grams) kosher salt

2 to 3 tablespoons (30 to 45 milliliters) whole milk

1 tablespoon (3 grams) dried or fresh chives, chopped

Directions

Pancakes

1. Boil, drain, and mash the potatoes (see recipe page 32). Chill until cold or overnight.
2. In a small bowl, combine the flour, baking soda and salt. Set aside.
3. In a large bowl, add the cold mashed potatoes, grated potatoes, and flour mixture. Pour in the buttermilk and combine. If the mixture is too thick or dry, add more buttermilk.
4. In a heavy pan over medium-high heat, melt the butter. Scoop the potato mixture into the pan to form individual patties, pressing down to flatten them. Fry until the bottoms are nicely browned, then flip them over and fry the other side. Be careful not to cook them too fast or they will brown before the raw potato is cooked. Adjust the heat as needed.
5. Transfer the boxty to a warm oven while you fry the remaining patties. Serve immediately while hot.

Sour Cream and Chive Sauce

1. In a small bowl, stir together sour cream, onion powder, garlic powder, salt, milk (just enough to bring the sauce to a pourable consistency), and chives. Store refrigerated for up to one week.

Irish Breakfast – "Fry"

30 minutes

2 servings

Ingredients

1 or 2 Irish bacon slices

4 Irish Sausages (2 per person)

4 eggs

4 ounces (113 grams) baked beans

4 ounces (113 grams) mushrooms, chopped

1 tomato, halved

TIP

Irish bacon or "rashers" is leaner and typically thicker than American bacon. It's known for its savory flavor and tender bite.

Directions

1. In a large skillet, melt 1 tablespoon (15 milliliters) of butter.
2. Add rashers to the skillet, letting them fry in the butter until they are well cooked but not excessively crispy. Take the rashers off the heat, place on a plate and set the plate in a hot oven to keep them warm.
3. Use the same pan to cook the sausages and, once ready, put them with the rashers to keep warm.
4. Add the mushrooms and tomato halves to the pan; let everything cook, then set aside.
5. In a small pot over medium heat, cook the baked beans.
6. In the skillet, fry the eggs to your desired style.
7. Once everything is ready, place on a large plate (one per person) and serve hot with a side of white toast, butter, jam, orange juice, tea or coffee.

Breakfast Hash

30 minutes

4 servings

Ingredients

4 cups (600 grams) russet potatoes, peeled and diced

4 cups (900 grams) corned beef, cooked and chopped

6 tablespoons (90 milliliters) unsalted butter, divided

1 small sweet onion, diced

½ teaspoon (1.2 grams) kosher salt

½ teaspoon (2.3 grams) black pepper

½ teaspoon (2.8 grams) garlic powder

½ teaspoon (2.8 grams) onion powder

TIP

Great for a post St. Patrick's Day brunch to use your leftover Corned Beef and Cabbage

Directions

1. In a large pot, boil the potatoes just until fork tender, 5 to 10 minutes. Drain well.
2. In a large skillet over medium heat, add 4 tablespoons (60 milliliters) butter. Once melted, add the cooked potatoes, onion, salt, and pepper. Cook, occasionally stirring, until the onions are softened and the potatoes and onion start to brown, 8 to 10 minutes.
3. Add corned beef, garlic powder, and onion powder to the skillet. Stir until combined.
4. Using the back of a spatula, press the mixture down to form an even layer. Cook for 3 to 5 minutes or until a golden crust begins to form on the bottom.
5. Scrape the bottom of the pan and flip over the hash, so the crusty part is on top. Mix in the remaining 2 tablespoons (30 milliliters) butter.
6. Again, using the spatula, press the hash down to form an even layer. Cook another 3 to 5 minutes until golden on the bottom. Continue doing this until you reach your desired browning. Serve hot.

Fruit Scones

30 minutes

8 servings

Ingredients

1 cup (113 grams) flour

1 tablespoon (14 grams) baking powder

⅓ cup (80 grams) caster sugar

¼ teaspoon (1.5 grams) of salt

⅓ cup (80 milliliters) unsalted butter, diced

½ cup (57 grams) dried cranberries, or dried fruit of your choice

4 tablespoons (60 milliliters) milk

1 egg, beaten

Directions

1. Preheat oven to 425°F (220°C).
2. In a large bowl, add flour, baking powder, sugar, and salt and mix until combined.
3. Then, using your fingers, rub the butter in until the mixture is the consistency of powdery breadcrumbs, then add the dried fruit and mix again.
4. In a different bowl, whisk the egg and the milk.
5. Make a hole in the center of your dry ingredients and pour in your egg and milk mixture. To combine, use a knife at the start and then, once the dough starts coming together, your fingers. Move the dough onto a clean, floured kitchen counter and spread it until it is about 1 inch (2.5 cm) thick.
6. Use a cutter (or a large glass) to shape out as many scones as your dough allows, about 8 with this recipe. Use the scraps of dough to make one or two more scones.
7. Place the scones on a baking sheet close enough to each other that their sides touch.
8. Bake for about 8 minutes, then lower the temperature to 325°F (160°C) and bake for an additional 10 minutes or until they have fully risen and are golden.
9. Remove from the oven, cool on a rack and serve with your topping of choice.

TIP
Caster sugar has very fine crystals, making it dissolve more quickly than the larger crystals of granulated sugar.

Tea Brack

1 hour 55 minutes plus overnight soaking time

1 loaf

Ingredients

1 cup (240 milliliters) brewed hot tea

2 cups (480 milliliters) raisins

1½ cups (260 grams) dates, chopped

¾ cup (165 grams) light brown sugar, packed

2 cups (226 grams) whole wheat flour

1 tablespoon (14 grams) baking powder

½ teaspoon (3 grams) salt

1 large egg

1 tablespoon (12 grams) granulated sugar

Directions

1. Pour hot tea over raisins and dates. Let sit for at least 45 minutes, stirring occasionally to ensure all the fruit has a chance to soften and plump. Ideally, place the mixture in the fridge overnight.
2. In a large bowl, mix the brown sugar, flour, baking powder, salt, and fruit, along with the liquid they were soaking in.
3. Stir in the egg until everything is uniformly incorporated.
4. Spread in a greased 8-inch (20-centimeter) round cake pan and sprinkle with granulated sugar. Bake in a preheated 325°F (160°C) oven for 60 to 70 minutes.
5. Turn brack out of pan and cool on a wire rack.

Cheese Toasties

15 minutes

12 servings

Ingredients

1 baguette

2 ½ teaspoons (12.5 millimeters) Dijon mustard

2 ounces (27 grams) cheddar cheese, grated

¼ teaspoon (1 gram) cracked black pepper

Fresh thyme for garnish

Directions

1. Slice baguette into 12 rounds, roughly ½ inch (1.25 centimeters) thick; apply a smear of Dijon mustard on each.
2. Place toasts on a baking tray and sprinkle with cheese.
3. Broil or bake in a toaster oven until golden and cheese is melted.
4. Sprinkle with fresh thyme and a liberal amount of cracked black pepper.

Small Plates, Sides & Snacks

Potato Leek Soup

40 minutes

8 servings

Ingredients

8 tablespoons (120 milliliters) butter, divided, Irish salted butter recommended

3 large leeks, white and light green parts only, halved and sliced

2 pounds (907 grams) russet potatoes, peeled and diced

4 cups (960 milliliters) chicken stock, or vegetable broth for a vegetarian version

¼ teaspoon (0.7 grams) kosher salt

¼ teaspoon (1 gram) black pepper

chopped chives, bacon, and/or sour cream for serving (optional)

Directions

1. In a large pot over medium heat, melt 6 tablespoons (90 milliliters) of the butter.
2. Add the leeks; stir to coat in the butter. Cook for approximately 10 minutes over medium heat, stirring occasionally until the leeks are tender and soft.
3. Add the potatoes, broth, salt and pepper; bring to a boil.
4. Cover, reduce heat to low, and simmer for 10 to 15 minutes, until potatoes are cooked through and soft when pierced with a fork.
5. Use an immersion blender to purée the soup directly in the pot. Turn off heat and stir in the remaining 2 tablespoons (30 milliliters) of butter until melted.
6. Serve topped with chopped fresh chives, cracked black pepper, crumbled bacon, and/or sour cream, if desired.

TIP

If you don't have an immersion blender, you can blend it in batches using a standing blender, or you can use a potato masher.

Irish Omelette

15 minutes

2 servings

Ingredients

4 eggs, large

1 potato, cooked and mashed

1 tablespoon (15 milliliters) lemon juice

1 tablespoon (3 grams) chives, chopped

½ teaspoon (3 grams) salt

¼ teaspoon (1 gram) pepper

1 tablespoon (15 milliliters) butter

Directions

1. Separate the eggs. In a small bowl, beat the yolks and set aside.
2. In a large bowl, add mashed potato and egg yolks, mixing thoroughly, then add lemon juice, chives, salt and pepper.
3. Whisk the egg whites until stiff, then stir them into the potato mixture.
4. Melt the butter in a pan, add the potato mixture and cook until golden. Remove pan from heat and carefully place under the broiler to finish and puff it up. Serve immediately.

Baked Carrots and Parsnips

45 minutes

4 servings

Ingredients

1 pound (454 grams) carrots, peeled and cut into uniform sticks

1 pound (454 grams) parsnips, peeled and cut into uniform sticks

2 tablespoons (30 milliliters) olive oil

3 tablespoons (45 milliliters) honey

2 tablespoons (30 milliliters) butter, melted

1 tablespoon (2.4 grams) fresh thyme leaves or 1 teaspoon (1 gram) dried thyme

½ teaspoon (1.2 grams) kosher salt

¼ teaspoon (1.2 milliliters) freshly ground black pepper

Fresh parsley, chopped, for garnish (optional)

TIP
For even cooking and browning, stir the vegetables halfway through the roasting time.

Directions

1. Preheat the oven to 400°F (200°C) and line a large baking sheet with parchment paper.
2. To make the glaze, in a small bowl, whisk together the butter, honey, olive oil, thyme, salt, and pepper.
3. Place the carrots and parsnips in a large bowl. Pour the glaze over them and toss with your hands until the vegetables are well coated.
4. Spread the vegetables in a single layer on the baking sheet to ensure they roast evenly. Bake for 35 to 45 minutes, or until they are fork-tender and nicely browned.
5. Transfer the roasted carrots and parsnips to a serving dish. Garnish with fresh parsley before serving.

Colcannon

2 hours

6 servings

Ingredients

3 pounds (1,362 grams) of potatoes, scrubbed

1 cup (240 milliliters) butter, divided

1 ¼ cups (300 milliliters) milk, hot

¼ teaspoon (1 gram) black pepper

1 head cabbage, cored and finely shredded

4 scallions, finely chopped

Parsley, chopped for garnish

Directions

1. Steam the potatoes in their skins for 30 minutes. Peel them and chop with a knife before mashing.
2. In a large bowl, add the potatoes and mash thoroughly to remove all the lumps.
3. Add 8 tablespoons (120 milliliters) of butter in pieces. Gradually add milk, stirring constantly. Season with pepper.
4. In a large pot, add the cabbage and water to cover. Boil the cabbage unsalted until it turns a darker color. Add two tablespoons (30 milliliters) butter and cover with lid for two minutes. Drain thoroughly and chop into small pieces. Return to the pot.
5. Add cabbage and scallions to mashed potatoes, stirring gently.
6. Use an ice cream or cookie scooper and place a scoop of potatoes on the serving plate. Make an indentation on the top by swirling a wooden spoon. Put one tablespoon of butter into each indentation and sprinkle with parsley.

Mashed Potatoes

40 minutes

6 servings

Ingredients

3 pounds (1,362 grams) Russet potatoes

2 tablespoons (30 milliliters) whole milk

2 tablespoons butter (30 milliliters)

¼ teaspoon (1.5 grams) salt or to taste

3 tablespoons (45 milliliters) heavy cream

TIP

Boiling the potatoes with skins on makes it easier to peel off the skins once the potatoes have cooled.

Directions

1. Wash the potatoes; do not peel them.
2. Place the potatoes in a large pot. Cover with cold water and bring to a boil over high heat. Then, reduce the heat and allow to simmer for about 20 to 25 minutes until they are fork tender.
3. Strain the potatoes and allow them to cool slightly in a colander.
4. While the potatoes are cooling, add the milk and butter to a clean saucepan. Bring to a simmer over very low heat. Do not let the milk boil or your potatoes will have a scalded milk flavor. Turn the heat off under the milk and butter while peeling the potatoes.
5. Peel the boiled potatoes. Add them to the saucepan of hot milk and melted butter. Smash the potatoes with a potato masher. Season with salt and continue to mash to remove all the lumps.
6. Add about 2 to 4 tablespoons (30 to 45 milliliters) of the heavy cream and mix. The amount required depends on how floury and starchy the potatoes are. Do not add too much cream or the potatoes will become too loose.
7. Spoon into a large serving bowl or serve individual portions on each dinner plate.

Mini Shepherd's Pie

1 hour

6 Mini Pies

Ingredients

¼ pound (113 grams) ground lamb or ground beef

¼ cup (85 grams) white onion, finely diced

2 teaspoons (5.2 grams) all-purpose flour plus additional for rolling out pie crust

2 teaspoons (11 grams) tomato paste

¼ teaspoon (1 gram) kosher salt

¼ teaspoon (1 gram) ground black pepper

½ cup (120 milliliters) beef broth

½ teaspoon (0.5 grams) fresh thyme leaves

½ teaspoon (2.5 milliliters) Worcestershire sauce

½ cup (75 grams) frozen mixed peas and carrots

1 refrigerated pie crust

¾ cup (165 grams) mashed potatoes – see recipe page 32

¼ teaspoon (0.5 grams) ground paprika

Chopped fresh parsley for garnish (optional)

Directions

1. In a large skillet, place lamb or beef and onion over medium-high heat. Cook 6 to 8 minutes or until meat is cooked through, stirring occasionally and breaking up meat with side of spoon. Spoon off and discard any excess fat.
2. Stir in flour, tomato paste, salt and pepper; cook 1 minute, stirring constantly.
3. Stir in broth, thyme and Worcestershire; heat to boiling over medium-high heat.
4. Reduce to medium-low; simmer for 5 minutes or until mixture is thickened, stirring occasionally. Remove from heat; stir in peas and carrots.
5. Soften pie crust according to package directions.
6. Preheat oven to 375°F (190°C).
7. On lightly floured work surface, roll pie crust to a dimeter of 14 inches (35 centimeters) Using a 4.5-inch (11-centimeter) round cutter (or a small bowl), cut 6 rounds from crust.
8. Press each round into a muffin cup. Transfer to oven and bake for 10 to 11 minutes or until lightly browned.
9. Fill muffin cups with meat mixture.
10. If necessary, microwave mashed potatoes for 1 to 2 minutes or until warm and spreadable. Spread potatoes over meat mixture. Sprinkle with paprika. Transfer to oven and bake for 20 to 25 minutes or until potatoes are golden brown.
11. Served garnished with parsley, if desired.

Fish Cakes

40 minutes

6 servings

Ingredients

Fish Cakes

1 pound (454 grams) russett potatoes

1 pound (454 grams) cod fillet

1 tablespoon (15 grams) spicy ketchup or chili sauce

Fresh parsley, minced

Juice of ½ lemon

2 large eggs, beaten

½ teaspoon (2 grams) salt

½ teaspoon (1 gram) freshly ground black pepper

32 Ritz (buttery snack) crackers, finely crushed

8 tablespoons (120 milliliters) vegetable oil for frying

Green onion, sliced, for garnish

Parsley, chopped, for garnish

Tartar Sauce

1 pasteurized egg, room temperature

1 cup (240 milliliters) vegetable oil

1 teaspoon (5 milliliters) grainy Dijon mustard

Juice of ½ lemon

2 tablespoons (18 grams) capers

½ cup (70 grams) dill pickles, chopped

¼ teaspoon (1.5 grams) salt

¼ teaspoon (0.6 grams) fresh cracked pepper

TIP

You can keep well-wrapped fish cakes in the refrigerator for up to 24 hours prior to cooking.

Directions

Fish Cakes

1. Peel and chop the potatoes into large chunks. Put them in a saucepan, cover with cold water, add 2 teaspoons (10 milliliters) of salt, and bring to a boil. Cook until the potatoes are very soft.
2. Put the cod in a shallow sauté pan and cover with cold water. Bring to a boil, then cover, turn off the heat, and let the fish poach for about 10 to 15 minutes. Drain.
3. Drain the potatoes and put them into a large mixing bowl. Use the back of a fork to mash them, leaving a little bit of texture.
4. Add ketchup, parsley, lemon juice, beaten eggs, and salt and pepper. Stir briefly to combine, then add the fish, breaking it apart with your fingers as you add it. (Removing any tiny bones as you do this.) Fold the fish into the mixture until everything is evenly incorporated. It will be wet.
5. Shape the mixture into six equal patties. Flour your hands if necessary.
6. Roll each patty in the Ritz cracker crumbs, coating all surfaces, then set on a platter.
7. Coat the bottom of a skillet with vegetable oil and heat on medium until hot. Fry the cakes for about 5 minutes on each side until golden, crispy, and hot throughout. The fish cakes will be very delicate; move and flip them with extra care.
8. Serve immediately on top of a bed of greens with lots of fresh tartar sauce and lemon wedges on the side.

Tartar Sauce

1. Put all the ingredients into a jar that fits the head of your immersion blender. A 16-ounce (455-gram) Mason jar works best.
2. Set the head of the blender at the bottom of the jar and turn it on. Blend for a few seconds; as the sauce starts to thicken, gently raise the blender up to blend all the contents. This will only take a few seconds. You can pulse the blender a few times to continue to thicken the tartar sauce.
3. Remove the blender, give the sauce a stir, and taste to adjust the seasoning. Screw the cap on the jar and keep refrigerated until needed. Use within 7 to 10 days.

Vegetarian Stuffed Cabbage Rolls

45 minutes

8 Rolls

Ingredients

1 ½ cups (130 grams) fresh mushrooms, chopped

1 cup (124 grams) zucchini, diced

¾ cup (75 grams) green pepper, chopped

¾ cup (75 grams) sweet red pepper, chopped

¾ cup (175 milliliters) vegetable broth

½ cup (80 grams) bulgur

1 teaspoon (1 gram) dried basil

½ teaspoon (0.3 grams) dried marjoram

½ teaspoon (1 gram) dried thyme

¼ teaspoon (1 gram) pepper

1 large head cabbage

6 tablespoons (30 grams) Parmesan cheese, shredded and divided

2 teaspoons (10 milliliters) lemon juice

8 ounces (236 milliliters) tomato sauce

¼ teaspoon (1.2 milliliters) hot pepper sauce (optional)

Directions

1. In a large saucepan, combine the mushrooms, zucchini, green pepper, red pepper, broth, bulgur, basil, marjoram, thyme, and black pepper. Bring to a boil over medium heat. Reduce heat; cover and simmer for 5 minutes. Remove from the heat; let stand for 5 minutes.
2. Meanwhile, in a large pot, cook cabbage in boiling water just until leaves fall off head. Set aside 8 large leaves for rolls (refrigerate remaining cabbage for another use). Cut out the thick vein from each leaf, making a V-shape cut. Overlap cut ends before filling. Stir 4 tablespoons (28 grams) Parmesan cheese and lemon juice into vegetable mixture.
3. Place a heaping ⅓ cup (50 grams) of filling on each cabbage leaf; fold in sides. Starting at an unfolded edge, roll to completely enclose filling.
4. In a bowl, combine tomato sauce and hot pepper sauce; pour ⅓ cup (80 milliliters) into a 2-quart (2 liters) baking dish. Place cabbage rolls in dish and spoon remaining sauce over top. Cover and bake at 400°F (200°C) for 15 minutes or until heated through. Sprinkle with remaining Parmesan cheese.

Entrées

Beef Stew

1 hour 40 minutes

6 servings

Ingredients

2 ¾ pounds (1,247 grams) boneless beef chuck roast, cut into bite sized pieces

1 tablespoon (15 milliliters) olive oil

2 tablespoons (30 milliliters) butter

2 large shallots, chopped

2 celery stalks, chopped

3 carrots, peeled and chopped

3 garlic cloves, minced

3 Yukon gold potatoes, cut into 1-inch (2.5-centimeter) pieces

2 tablespoons (15 grams) flour

2 sprigs fresh rosemary

½ teaspoon (1.4 grams) dried thyme

2 bay leaves

5 cups (1,200 millimeters) beef or vegetable broth

1 teaspoon (5 grams) kosher salt, divided

¼ teaspoon (1 gram) pepper

Directions

1. In a large Dutch oven, add olive oil and turn to medium-high heat.
2. Season beef with kosher salt and black pepper. Add beef to pan in batches, leaving enough space to brown on all sides, about 5 to 6 minutes total. Repeat with any leftover meat.
3. Remove the meat and leave the drippings. Add butter, shallots, celery, and carrots. Stir occasionally over medium heat until softened, about 3 minutes. Add garlic and mix into the vegetables, then add the potatoes and beef. Stir in flour with a wood spoon until fully mixed in, coating all the beef and vegetables.
4. Stir in rosemary, thyme, bay leaves, ½ teaspoon (2.5 grams) kosher salt, and all the broth; reduce heat to low. Cover and cook for about 1½ hours, or until the beef is tender and flavors have combined. Taste and adjust any seasonings.
5. Remove bay leaves and rosemary stalks before serving.

Seafood Pie

1 hour 40 minutes

6 servings

Ingredients

½ cup (120 milliliters) butter, unsalted

1 ½ cups (180 grams) yellow onion, thinly sliced

1 cup (90 grams) fennel, thinly sliced

1 cup (100 grams) celery, thinly sliced

1 cup (122 grams) carrots, thinly sliced

½ cup (60 grams) all-purpose flour

3 ½ cups (840 milliliters) fish stock

¼ cup (120 milliliters) heavy cream, divided

1 tablespoon (10 grams) kosher salt

½ teaspoon (2.84 grams) ground black pepper

8-ounce (224 grams) halibut filet, skin removed, cut into 1-inch (2.5-centimeter) pieces

½ pound (227 grams) sea scallops, halved horizontally

½ pound (227 grams) medium shrimp, peeled and deveined

1 pound (454 grams) jumbo lump crabmeat

1 cup (140 grams) frozen green peas

2 tablespoons (8 grams) chopped fresh parsley, plus more for garnish

1 large egg, lightly beaten

1 package frozen puff pastry sheets, thawed

Directions

1. In a large saucepan over medium-high heat, melt butter. Add onion, fennel, celery, and carrots; cook, stirring often, until vegetables are softened and onion is translucent, about 8 minutes. Add flour and stir to coat vegetables well, stirring for 1 minute. Add fish stock and 3 tablespoons (45 milliliters) cream, stirring until mixture thickens into a creamy sauce, about 5 minutes. Season with salt and pepper, then gently fold in seafood, green peas and parsley.
2. Reduce heat to medium-low, and, gently stirring often, bring mixture to a low simmer until sauce is warm again, but the seafood will not be completely cooked through, about 6 to 8 minutes. Ladle 2 cups (480 milliliters) of the mixture into each ungreased ramekins or ovenproof bowls. Place bowls on a foil-lined rimmed baking sheet.
3. Preheat oven to 375°F (190°C) with a rack in the middle.
4. In a small bowl, whisk egg and remaining 1 tablespoon (15 milliliters) heavy cream. Place defrosted puff pastry sheets on a lightly floured work surface. Roll each sheet into a 13" x 13" (22.5 x 22.5 centimeter) square and cut each square into quarters. Discard any extra pastry. Place a square of pastry over each bowl, decoratively folding corners in to fit the bowl, and brush the top with egg wash.
5. Carefully use the tip of a knife to create 3 small slits in the center of the pastry to allow steam to vent during cooking. You may place chopped fennel fronds or parsley leaves on the top of the pastry, lightly pressing leaves onto the pastry in the egg wash to adhere.
6. Place baking sheet with individual portions in the preheated oven and bake until pastry is golden brown and filling is hot and bubbly, about 40 minutes. Let cool 10 minutes before serving.

Shepherd's Pie

1 hour 10 minutes

6 servings

Ingredients

Meat Filling

2 tablespoons (30 milliliters) olive oil

1 cup (150 grams) chopped yellow onion

1 pound (454 grams) ground beef or ground lamb

2 teaspoons (1 gram) dried parsley leaves

1 teaspoon (1 gram) dried rosemary leaves

1 teaspoon (1 gram) dried thyme leaves

½ teaspoon (1.2 grams) salt

½ teaspoon (3 grams) ground black pepper

1 tablespoon (15 milliliters) Worcestershire sauce

2 garlic cloves, minced

2 tablespoons (15 grams) all-purpose flour

2 tablespoons (32 grams) tomato paste

1 cup (240 milliliters) beef broth

1 cup (160 grams) frozen mixed peas & carrots

½ cup (75 grams) frozen corn kernels

Potato Topping

See Mashed Potato recipe on page 32

Directions

1. Preheat oven to 400°F (200°C).
2. In a large skillet, add the oil and place it over medium-high heat for 2 minutes. Add the onions. Cook 5 minutes, stirring occasionally.
3. Add the ground beef (or ground lamb) to the skillet, breaking it apart with a wooden spoon. Add the parsley, rosemary, thyme, salt, and pepper. Stir well. Cook for 6 to 8 minutes, until the meat is browned, stirring occasionally.
4. Add the Worcestershire sauce and garlic; stir to combine. Cook for 1 minute.
5. Add the flour and tomato paste. Stir until well incorporated and no clumps of tomato paste remain.
6. Add the broth, frozen peas and carrots, and frozen corn. Bring the liquid to a boil, then reduce to a simmer. Simmer for 5 minutes, stirring occasionally. Remove from heat and set aside.
7. Pour the meat mixture into a 9 x 9 inch (23 x 23 centimeter) baking dish. Spread it out into an even layer. Spoon the mashed potatoes on top of the meat, carefully spreading into an even layer.
8. If the baking dish looks very full, place it on a rimmed baking sheet so that the filling doesn't bubble over into your oven. Bake uncovered for 25 to 30 minutes. Cool for 15 minutes before serving.

Bangers and Mash

25 minutes

4 servings

Ingredients

1 tablespoon (7.5 milliliters) olive oil

8 pork sausage links

2 tablespoons (30 milliliters) butter, unsalted

1 large, sweet onion, halved and thinly sliced

2 cloves garlic, minced

3 tablespoons (23 grams) all-purpose flour

2 cups (480 milliliters) beef broth

¼ teaspoon (1.5 grams) salt

¼ teaspoon (1 gram) pepper

15 ounces (425 grams) sweet baby peas, for serving

TIP

For a traditional Irish Banger and Mash, use thick pork sausages, ideally a high-quality Irish banger, or a substitute a bratwurst or any other fatty pork sausage.

Directions

1. In a large nonstick skillet, warm olive oil over medium heat. Once hot, add sausage links.
2. Cook the sausage links until browned all over and cooked through (rolling frequently to prevent burning), about 10 to 12 minutes. Transfer to a paper towel-lined plate and pour off all but 1 tablespoon fat from the skillet.
3. Add butter to the skillet. Once bubbly, add the onion; stir to coat.
4. Continue to cook the onions for about 10 minutes until they're translucent, golden, and begin to caramelize.
5. Add garlic and cook until fragrant, about 20 seconds.
6. Add flour and mix through until completely combined and flour is dissolved.
7. Add ¾ cup (175 milliliters) of broth and stir into the onion so it becomes a sludge. Then add remaining broth and mix until combined. Simmer, stirring, until the gravy thickens but is slightly thinner than you want – it will thicken more as it sits.
8. Season with salt and pepper; serve on plate with peas and mashed potatoes (recipe page 32).

Roasted Salmon

30 minutes + marinating time

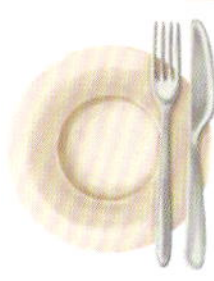

4 servings

Ingredients

3 tablespoons (45 milliliters) honey

3 tablespoons (45 milliliters) lemon juice

1 teaspoon (5 milliliters) lemon zest

3 teaspoons (3 grams) fresh thyme, chopped

2 tablespoons (30 milliliters) extra virgin olive oil

4 6-ounce (170-gram) salmon fillets

1 tablespoon (15 milliliters) butter

Directions

1. In a large sealable bag, add honey, lemon juice, thyme, lemon zest and olive oil. Close and shake to combine. Add salmon to bag and marinate 4 to 6 hours in the refrigerator.
2. Preheat oven to 450°F (230°C). Remove salmon from marinade and place on a foil-lined sheet pan. Sprinkle with sea salt and freshly ground pepper.
3. In a small saucepan, bring the marinade to a simmer. Simmer for 4 to 5 minutes or until reduced by half, the mixture will be syrupy. Add butter and swirl pan until butter is melted. Add the 1 teaspoon (5 milliliters) chopped fresh thyme.
4. Place pan with salmon in the oven and roast for 10 to 12 minutes, basting with the sauce halfway through.
5. Carefully place the salmon under broiler for the last few minutes if you like a more golden exterior. This is not necessary but makes for a more attractive appearance.
6. Transfer salmon to serving plates or platter and drizzle with sauce. Sprinkle with extra thyme, for garnish.

Corned Beef and Cabbage

4 hours 45 minutes

4 servings

Ingredients

5 ½ pounds (2,500 grams) corned beef brisket

2 large onions

10 carrots, cut into 1-inch (2.5-centimeter) pieces

2 heads cabbage, cored and cut into wedges

15 small white potatoes

Directions

1. Rinse brisket under cold water and place in a large pot. Add enough water to cover roast by 6 inches (15 centimeters).
2. Peel onions and place them in the pot. Bring to a boil; cook for about 30 minutes at a rolling boil. Reduce heat to medium-low, so water is at a gentle boil. Cover and cook for 3 ½ hours.
3. Remove onions and cut them into wedges, then return them to the pot. Add carrots, then place cabbage over roast. Place potatoes on top of cabbage. Cover and cook until potatoes are tender, about 30 minutes more. The potatoes should be immersed in the water by now, but if not, keep the lid on so they can steam.
4. Remove vegetables from the pot and place in a separate serving bowl. Keep corned beef in the pot until ready to slice and serve to prevent it from drying out too quickly.

Chicken with Mushroom Sauce

30 minutes

4 servings

Ingredients

4 boneless, skinless chicken breasts
2 tablespoons (30 milliliters) olive oil
1 medium yellow onion, finely chopped
3 cloves garlic, minced
8 ounces (227 grams) cremini mushrooms, sliced
1 cup (240 milliliters) chicken broth
½ cup (120 milliliters) heavy cream, room temperature
2 tablespoons (8 grams) fresh parsley, chopped
1 teaspoon (0.5 grams) fresh thyme leaves
¼ teaspoon (1.5 grams) salt
¼ teaspoon (1 gram) black pepper

Directions

1. Pat chicken breasts completely dry with paper towels and season both sides generously with salt and pepper.
2. In a large skillet over medium-high, heat oil until it shimmers, about 2 minutes.
3. Place chicken breasts in the hot skillet and cook for 6 to 7 minutes until golden brown on the bottom.
4. Flip chicken and cook another 6 to 7 minutes until internal temperature reaches 165°F (74°C).

5. Transfer chicken to a plate and cover to keep warm.
6. Reduce heat to medium and add onion to the same skillet.
7. Cook onions for 4 to 5 minutes until translucent and slightly softened.
8. Add garlic and cook for one minute until fragrant but not browned.
9. Add sliced mushrooms and cook for 8 to 10 minutes until they release their liquid and turn golden brown.
10. Pour in chicken broth, scraping up any browned bits from the bottom of the pan.
11. Simmer the broth mixture for 5 minutes until reduced by about half.
12. Stir in heavy cream and fresh thyme, then simmer for 3 to 4 minutes until sauce thickens slightly. The sauce should coat the back of a spoon; if too thin, continue to simmer a minute longer.
13. Return chicken to the skillet and spoon sauce over the top, heating through for 2 to 3 minutes until chicken is warmed.
14. Stir in fresh parsley just before serving.

Fish & Chips

30 minutes

4 to 6 servings

Ingredients

2 pounds (908 grams) cod, fresh or frozen

1 ¼ cups (150 grams) all-purpose flour, divided

½ cup (60 grams) cornstarch, divided

1 teaspoon (4 grams) baking powder

2 cups (480 milliliters) club soda

1 teaspoon (6 grams) salt

Oil (for frying)

3 large potatoes, peeled and cut into ½-inch (1.25-centimeter) fries

Directions

1. Place the cut potatoes into a medium bowl and cover with water for 30 minutes.
2. While the potatoes soak, prepare the fish batter.
3. In a large bowl, mix 1 cup (120 grams) flour, ¼ cup (30 grams) cornstarch, baking powder and salt.

TIP

Replace the club soda with non-alcoholic ginger beer to add a unique flavor.

4. Stir in enough club soda to make a batter about the consistency of thin pancake batter—not too thick, just thick enough to nicely coat a spoon.
5. Season the batter to taste, if desired, with seasoning of your choice.
6. In another bowl, mix remaining ¼ cup (30 grams) flour and ¼ cup (30 grams) cornstarch.
7. Cut fish into portion sizes and remove any pin bones; pat dry.
8. Remove potatoes from water and pat dry with a paper towel.
9. In heavy-bottomed Dutch oven, heat two quarts (2liters) oil over medium heat to 350°F (175°C); use a candy thermometer if you need to.
10. Carefully add potatoes to hot oil and increase heat to high. Fry, stirring with a slotted metal spoon, until fries turn light golden and just begin to brown at corners, 6 to 8 minutes.
11. Transfer fries (chips) to paper towels to drain.
12. Increase temperature of oil to 375°F (190°C). Oil in pan should be about 3 to 4 inches (15 to 20 centimeters) deep.
13. Dredge the fish in the dry flour/cornstarch mixture. Shake off any excess; this allows the batter to stick to the fish.
14. Dip dredged fish into batter, allowing any excess to drip off before carefully adding the fish to the hot oil.
15. Cook the fish one or two pieces at a time until golden brown.
16. Drain on paper towels on a cooling rack.
17. Serve while hot with chips.

Vegetarian Lentil Shepherd's Pie

1 hour 20 minutes

6 servings

Ingredients

Lentil Shepherd's Pie Filling

¾ cup (144 grams) dried green lentils

5 cups (1,200 milliliters) water, divided

1 ½ cup (355 milliliters) vegetable broth

4 sprigs fresh thyme

2 tablespoons (30 milliliters) unsalted butter

1 medium yellow onion, thinly sliced

8 ounces (224 grams) cremini mushrooms, thinly sliced

2 large cloves garlic, minced

2 medium carrots, peeled and diced

¾ cup (80 grams) sliced cauliflower florets

2 tablespoons (32 grams) tomato paste

½ teaspoon (2.8 grams) dried thyme

Potato Topping

20 ounces (570 grams) russet potatoes, peeled and cubed

16 ounces (454 grams) cauliflower, cut into large florets

1 ½ teaspoons (4.2 grams) kosher salt, plus more to taste

1 rosemary sprig (optional)

4 tablespoons (60 milliliters) unsalted butter, softened at room temperature

½ cup (120 milliliters) "lite" coconut milk

¼ teaspoon (1 gram) freshly cracked black pepper

TIP

This recipe has cauliflower added to the mashed potatoes. If you prefer traditional mashed potatoes, refer to recipe on page 32.

Directions

1. Rinse the lentils. In a large pot, bring 2 ½ cups (540 milliliters) of water to a boil. Reduce to a simmer and add the lentils, vegetable paste, and sprigs of fresh thyme.
2. Cover and simmer until the lentils are tender, about 20 minutes. Check on the pot periodically to ensure the liquid doesn't completely boil off. Add another ½ cup (120 milliliters) of water if needed. Set aside.
3. While the lentils cook, in a large skillet, melt the butter over medium-high heat. Add the sliced onions and sauté until they are lightly browned. Reduce heat to medium and continue to cook until parts of the onions are darker brown, about 20 minutes.
4. Add the mushrooms and continue to sauté for another 15 minutes. The entire mixture will be deeply aromatic with the caramelization, and a brown coating will develop on the bottom of the pan.
5. Add the broth and simmer for a few minutes until most of it has been absorbed or cooked off. Add the remaining 2 ½ cups (540 milliliters) of water and stir in 2 teaspoons (10 milliliters) of the paste. Bring to a low simmer.
6. Add the carrots, cauliflower, tomato paste, and dried thyme. Simmer until the carrots are tender. Add the lentils and any remaining liquid.

Potato Topping

1. Place the potatoes and cauliflower florets in a large saucepan or Dutch oven and add just enough water to cover. Add salt and stir to combine. Place the rosemary sprig on top. Bring to a boil and cook until both potatoes and cauliflower are fork tender and are very soft when poked, about 15 minutes.
2. Thoroughly drain the potatoes and cauliflower in a colander and discard the rosemary sprig. Pat the potatoes dry with paper towels or a clean dish towel. Squeeze out excess water from the cauliflower.
3. Return potatoes and cauliflower to the saucepan. Add the softened butter, lite coconut milk, and salt and pepper. Mash everything together using a handheld potato masher or an immersion blender. Taste for seasonings, adding more salt as needed.
4. Preheat the oven to 375°F (190°C). If your skillet is ovenproof and has enough space, leave the Lentil Filling in there. If not, transfer it to a large (3 quart/3 liter) baking dish.
5. Smooth the Lentil Filling out. Then, spoon and carefully spread out the mashed potato topping on top, covering the whole surface.
6. Bake for 20 minutes, or until the lentil filling starts to bubble up. Remove from the oven and turn on the broiler. Carefully place the pan under the broiler for a few minutes until the crust is golden brown. To finish, drizzle with more olive oil and garnish with fresh parsley, if desired.

Desserts

Kerry Apple Cake with Custard Sauce

1 hour 50 minutes

16 Servings

Ingredients

Cake

3 cups (339 grams) Honeycrisp or Granny Smith apples, peeled and diced

1 tablespoon (15 milliliters) lemon juice

3 ⅓ cups (400 grams) all-purpose flour

4 ½ teaspoons (22 grams) baking powder

¾ teaspoon (4.5 grams) salt

1 teaspoon (2.6 grams) cinnamon

⅛ teaspoon (0.7 grams) nutmeg

1 ¼ cups (300 milliliters) unsalted butter, softened

1 ½ cups (300 grams) plus 1 tablespoon (12.5 grams) granulated sugar, divided

4 large eggs, room temperature

1 ½ teaspoons (7.5 milliliters) vanilla extract

2 tablespoons (25 grams) raw cane sugar

Custard Sauce

⅓ cup (65 grams) granulated sugar

3 large egg yolks

¼ teaspoon (1.5 grams) salt

¾ cup (175 milliliters) whole milk

¾ cup (175 milliliters) heavy cream

1 ½ teaspoons (7.5 milliliters) vanilla bean paste

TIP

Using a metal bowl is beneficial because it allows the sauce to be cooled efficiently in an ice bath, stopping the cooking process and preventing the eggs from scrambling.

Directions

Cake

1. Preheat the oven to 350°F (175°C) with a rack in the middle. Spray a 9-inch (23-centimeter) springform pan with nonstick cooking spray. Line the bottom with parchment paper and give it one more spray.
2. In a large bowl, add apples, 1 tablespoon (12 grams) sugar, and lemon juice. Toss and set aside.
3. In a large bowl, whisk together flour, baking powder, salt, cinnamon, and nutmeg. Set aside.
4. In a medium bowl, add the butter and remaining 1 ½ cups (300 grams) sugar; mix until well combined, scraping the sides of the bowl as needed. Add eggs, one at a time, making sure they are incorporated before adding the next. Add vanilla and combine.
5. Add the flour mixture to the butter mixture and make sure to stop mixing once it's just combined.
6. Stir in the apples with a spatula. Do not overmix. Spread batter into the prepared pan and sprinkle with sugar.
7. Bake on the center rack for 30 minutes, then cover the cake with foil to keep it from overbrowning. Bake an additional 30 to 45 minutes, until a toothpick inserted in the middle comes out clean. Cool on a wire rack for 10 minutes, then release the cake from the pan.

Custard Sauce

1. Place a fine-mesh sieve over a medium bowl. Fill a large bowl with ice water and put aside.
2. In a medium metal bowl, whisk together the sugar, egg yolks, and salt.
3. In a saucepan, heat the milk and cream over medium-low until steaming. Do not let it boil.
4. Add the heated milk/cream to the egg mixture gradually, so as not to scramble the eggs. Return the mixture to the saucepan; cook over medium-low heat, stirring constantly, until the mixture thickens and coats the back of a spoon, about 8 to 10 minutes.
5. Strain the custard through the sieve, then place the bowl of strained custard into the bowl of ice water; whisk until the mixture is about 70°F (21°C). Add vanilla bean paste. Loosely cover and refrigerate until chilled (about 3 to 4 hours).

Shortbread Cookies

1 hour 15 minutes

30 cookies

Ingredients

1 ½ cups (360 milliliters) butter, softened

¾ cup (150 grams) superfine sugar

1 tablespoon (15 milliliters) vanilla extract

2 ½ cups (300 grams) flour

½ teaspoon (2.5 milliliters) salt

2 tablespoons (8 grams) sugar for dusting

Directions

1. Preheat the oven to 350°F (175°C). Set out a 9 x 13-inch (23 x 33-centimeter) baking pan and line with parchment paper.
2. In a large bowl, beat the softened butter and superfine sugar, scraping the sides of the bowl to make sure they are well mixed.
3. Add the vanilla and beat it into the butter and sugar.

TIP

Be sure to let the shortbread cool completely in the pan before serving or the buttery cookies will crumble when you try to lift them out.

4. In a separate mixing bowl, combine the flour and salt, then add to the butter mixture. Stir until well combined.
5. Press the prepared dough into the baking pan. The dough will be quite sticky, so it helps to slightly dampen your hands and pat it into place.
6. Sprinkle the last 2 tablespoons (25 grams) of sugar over the top of the shortbread.
7. Bake for 1 hour or until lightly golden brown.
8. Give the shortbread 3 to 4 minutes to cool, then use a paring knife to score the dough. Slice the dough into 3 long equal strips (2 cuts each ⅓ of the way into the width of the dough). Then slice the dough crosswise so each shortbread cookie is about 1 inch (2.5 centimeters) wide. You'll make about 10 cuts which will form 33 long, rectangular cookies.
9. Once the cookies have been sliced, use the tines of a fork to gently poke holes in the surface of each cookie in an even pattern.

Leprechaun Hat Rainbow Cake

1 hour 50 minutes

12 servings

Ingredients

Rainbow Cake Layers

5 cups (600 grams) all-purpose flour

3 cups (600 grams) granulated sugar

1 tablespoon (14 grams) baking powder

½ teaspoon (3 grams) baking soda

1 teaspoon (5 grams) salt

6 large eggs, room temperature

1½ cups (360 milliliters) vegetable oil

1½ cups (360 milliliters) whole milk

1 tablespoon (15 milliliters) vanilla extract

Food coloring (red, yellow, blue, green, orange, and purple)

Buttercream

2½ cups (560 milliliters) unsalted butter, softened

½ teaspoon (2 grams) salt

10 cups (1,200 grams) confectioners' sugar

½ cup (120 milliliters) heavy cream, room temperature

2 teaspoons (10 milliliters) vanilla extract

Directions

Cake

1. Preheat the oven to 350°F (175°C). Grease two or three 8-inch (20-centimeter) round cake pans with baking spray or butter. Line the bottoms with parchment paper.
2. In a large mixing bowl, whisk together the flour, sugar, baking powder, baking soda, and salt.
3. In another large mixing bowl, combine the eggs, vegetable oil, milk, and vanilla; whisk until well combined. Pour into the flour mixture and whisk until combined.
4. Divide the batter among 6 mixing bowls. Use food coloring to make red, orange, yellow, green, blue, and purple batters. Pour a single-color batter into each cake pan. Place the remaining batter bowls in the fridge until ready to bake.
5. Bake for 20 minutes or until a toothpick inserted in the center comes out clean. Let the cakes cool for 10 minutes in the pan, then remove and finish cooling on a wire rack.
6. Wash the pans, grease and line with parchment paper again, and bake the remaining batters.
7. If the tops of your rainbow cake layers are domed then use a serrated knife to carefully cut off the top of the domes so you can stack them evenly.

Buttercream

1. In a large mixing bowl, beat the butter and salt until very fluffy and pale, about 5 minutes.
2. Gradually add the confectioners' sugar 1 cup (120 grams) at a time, adding 1 tablespoon (15 milliliters) of cream at a time, stirring continuously. Stop and scrape down the bowl occasionally during mixing. Once all the sugar is added, beat in the vanilla and add additional cream if the frosting feels grainy when rubbed between your fingers. Continue to beat until light and fluffy, about 1 minute.

Assemble the Cake

1. Once the cakes are cooled, flip one over and put it on a cardboard cake round; spread some frosting on it before flipping over the other cakes and doing the same.
2. Remove the parchment paper from the cake layers. Place the purple layer on a cake plate and spread ½ cup (120 milliliters) of frosting over the top. Place the blue layer on top and spread another ½ cup (120 milliliters) of frosting on top. Repeat with the remaining cake layers in the order of green, yellow, orange, and red.

To Decorate the Leprechaun Hat

1. You can add green, yellow, and black food coloring to the buttercream frosting and frost the cake entirely in green, adding a black belt with a yellow buckle.
2. Or as shown in photo, cover the cake with green fondant to give the Leprechaun hat a shiny and smooth finish. You'll need green, black, and white (or gold) fondant.
3. Frost the entire cake and make it really smooth.
4. Cover the cake with green fondant.
5. Cut out a green fondant hat brim on a cake board or cake plate. Set the fondant-covered cake in the center of the green hat brim. Add a black fondant hat band and make a buckle. You can simply make the buckle out of yellow fondant, or you can spray a white or yellow buckle with gold food-coloring spray.

TIP

Make sure to allow the cake layers to cool before you add the buttercream. The longer you chill the rainbow cake, the better the buttercream will stick to the cake layers.

Blackberry Sorbet

18 minutes

4 servings

Ingredients

2 cups (300 grams) fresh blackberries, rinsed, stalks removed

½ cup (100 grams) sugar

½ cup (120 milliliters) water

2 egg whites

Directions

1. Purée the blackberries in a blender and strain through a sieve.
2. In a saucepan, dissolve the sugar in the water and boil for about 5 minutes to make a syrup. Add the blackberries and boil for one minute. Set aside to cool.
3. In a small bowl, beat the egg whites.
4. When the liquid has cooled, fold it into stiffly beaten egg whites.
5. Freeze the mixture in an ice cream machine or in a tray in the freezer. If freezing in a tray, stir the mixture about once an hour to prevent large ice crystals from developing.

Tea Cake

1 hour 15 minutes

10 servings

Ingredients

1 cup (200 grams) sugar

½ cup (120 milliliters) butter, softened

2 large eggs

1 ½ teaspoons (7.5 milliliters) vanilla extract

1 ¾ cups (210 grams) all-purpose flour

2 teaspoons (8 grams) baking powder

½ teaspoon (2 grams) salt

½ cup (120 milliliters) milk, or more if needed

¼ cup (30 grams) confectioners' sugar for dusting

Directions

1. Preheat the oven to 350°F (170°C). Grease and flour a 9-inch (23-centimeter) round pan.
2. In a large bowl, cream sugar and butter together until light and fluffy. Beat in eggs, one at a time, mixing until fully incorporated after each addition. Stir in vanilla.
3. In a medium bowl, combine flour, baking powder, and salt.
4. Stir dry ingredients into wet ingredients alternately with milk, adding 1 to 2 tablespoons (15 to 30 milliliters) more milk if batter is too stiff.
5. Spread batter evenly into the prepared pan.
6. Bake until a toothpick inserted in the center comes out clean, 30 to 35 minutes. Cool in the pan on a wire rack for 10 minutes.
7. Turn cake out onto a serving plate and cool to room temperature, 20 to 30 minutes. Dust with confectioners' sugar right before serving.

Rhubarb Crumble

30 minutes

8 servings

Ingredients

Crumble

1 cup (125 grams) all-purpose flour

½ cup (110 grams) light brown sugar

1¼ cups (106 grams) rolled oats, or Irish oatmeal if available

8 tablespoons (120 milliliters) butter

Rhubarb Base

4 cups (500 grams) rhubarb, washed, trimmed and chopped

⅓ cup (67 grams) sugar

3 tablespoons (45 milliliters) water

½ teaspoon (2 grams) ground ginger, optional

Directions

1. Preheat oven to 375°F (190°C). Lightly grease a 2-quart (2-liter) ovenproof pie dish with butter.
2. In a saucepan, add the chopped rhubarb, sugar and water. Bring to a boil and simmer for about 8 to 10 minutes, until the rhubarb starts to soften but does not lose its shape. Add the ground ginger if desired and stir.
3. While the rhubarb is simmering, make the crumble. In a medium bowl, add the flour, light brown sugar and oats. Add the butter; using your fingertips, rub the butter into the dry ingredients.
4. Transfer the partially cooked rhubarb to the greased pie dish.
5. Evenly spread the crumble mixture over rhubarb base.
6. Bake for 20 minutes, until the top is golden brown.
7. Serve with freshly whipped cream or a scoop of ice cream.

Lace Cookies

20 minutes

10 servings

Ingredients

½ cup (60 milliliters) butter, melted

¾ cup (150 grams) white sugar

1 large egg, beaten

1 cup (80 grams) quick cooking oats

3 tablespoons (23 grams) all-purpose flour

1 teaspoon (5 milliliters) vanilla extract

¼ teaspoon (1.5 grams) salt

¼ teaspoon (1 gram) baking powder

Directions

1. Preheat the oven to 350°F (175°C). Line a baking sheet with parchment paper.
2. In a large bowl, add butter and sugar; stir to combine. Add beaten egg and mix well. Stir in oats, flour, vanilla, salt, and baking powder.
3. Drop spoonfuls of dough onto the prepared baking sheet about 3 inches (7.5 centimeters) apart, as the dough will spread.
4. Bake until edges are golden brown, about 8 minutes.
5. Let cool completely before removing cookies from the baking sheet.

Ginger Snaps

35 minutes

24 servings

Ingredients

¾ cup (175 millimeters) butter, unsalted

1 cup (220 grams) brown sugar

1 egg, large

¼ teaspoon (1.5 grams) salt

2 cups (250 grams) all-purpose flour

½ teaspoon (3 grams) baking soda

1 teaspoon (2.3 grams) ground cloves

2 teaspoons (4 grams) ground ginger

1 teaspoon (2.6 grams) cinnamon

½ cup (60 grams) confectioners' sugar

Directions

1. Preheat the oven to 350°F (175°C) and line a baking sheet with parchment paper.
2. In a large bowl, combine butter and brown sugar until light and fluffy.
3. Add egg and salt; stir until combined.
4. Add in flour, baking soda, cloves, ginger, and cinnamon. Mix until just combined.
5. Using a 1-tablespoon (15-milliliter) scoop, divide the batter into 24 even portions. Shape into balls and roll in confectioners' sugar until coated all over. Place the balls on the prepared baking sheet about 1½ inches (3.75 centimeters) apart.
6. Bake for about 10 to 12 minutes (or slightly longer if you like them more crispy).

Chocolate Mint Cupcakes

35 minutes

12 to 16 cupcakes

Ingredients

Cupcakes

¾ cup (94 grams) all-purpose flour

½ cup (55 grams) unsweetened cocoa powder

¾ teaspoon (3 grams) baking powder

½ teaspoon (3 grams) baking soda

¼ teaspoon (1.5 grams) salt

½ cup (100 grams) granulated sugar

½ cup (110 grams) packed light brown sugar

⅓ cup (78 milliliters) vegetable or canola oil

2 teaspoons (10 milliliters) pure vanilla extract

1 teaspoon (5 milliliters) pure mint extract

2 large eggs, room temperature

½ cup buttermilk (118 milliliters), room temperature

Mint Buttercream Frosting

1 ⅔ cups (394 milliliters) unsalted butter, softened

3 ½ cups (420 grams) confectioners' sugar

½ teaspoon (3 grams) sugar

3 tablespoons (45 milliliters) heavy cream

1 ¼ teaspoons (6 milliliters) vanilla extract

1 ¼ teaspoons (6 milliliters) peppermint extract

Directions

Cupcakes

1. Preheat oven to 350°F (177°C). Line a 12-cup muffin pan with cupcake liners and a second pan with a few extra liners if needed.
2. In a medium bowl, whisk together the flour, cocoa powder, baking powder, baking soda, and salt.
3. In a large bowl, whisk together granulated sugar, brown sugar, oil, vanilla, mint extract, and eggs until smooth. Whisk in the buttermilk until well combined.
4. Add the dry ingredients to the wet mixture and whisk just until combined. Do not overmix; the batter will be thin.
5. Divide batter evenly among cupcake liners, filling each about two-thirds full.
6. Bake 18 to 20 minutes, or until a toothpick inserted in the center comes out clean.
7. Let cupcakes cool in the pan for 5 minutes, then transfer to a wire rack to cool completely before frosting.
8. Frost cupcakes and top with chocolate savings, chocolate chips, or green sprinkles.

Mint Buttercream Frosting

1. Using a stand mixer fitted with a whisk attachment, whip butter on medium-high speed until smooth and creamy, about 20 seconds.
2. Add sugars and salt; mix on medium-low speed until most of the sugar is moistened, about 45 seconds.
3. Scrape down the bowl. Add cream, vanilla extract, and peppermint extract, then whip on medium-high speed until light, fluffy, and pale—about 4 minutes. Scrape down the bowl as needed.

Irish Folklore

Folklore is the collection of shared traditions, beliefs, and stories passed down through generations by word of mouth. These stories are often presented as if they happened, even if their truth is debatable. Irish folklore has a vast array of unique creatures from delightful and real animals to scary and supernatural fairies. It's no surprise that their lore has continued to be told for hundreds and thousands of years.

Faries (or, in Gaelic, the Aos Si')—also known as "little people," "wee folk," faerie, and fay—are among Ireland's most revered mythological creatures. They are not the cute, winged fairies from storybooks; Irish fairies are described as being demoted angels, demons, or spirits of the dead. These supernatural beings usually appear to look like humans on a tiny scale and are powerful immortal spirits who are dangerous and can bring misfortune or death to humans who interfere with them. The Irish were so fearful of angering the fairies that they often avoided referring to them directly by name, instead using flattering terms like "the good people" or "The Gentry." The belief was that fairies are invisible and always listening.

Many stories about fairies served as a warning to avoid danger, uphold Christian faith, and show respect for the natural world and the unseen forces within it. While some stories have happy endings, most Irish folklore is not designed to be cheerful: The core of Irish fairy folklore is defined by unpredictability, danger, and respect for the otherworldly. Often, folklore provided an answer for tragedies in a time without modern medicine.

While fairies could sometimes grant wishes, they were just as likely to cause misfortune. If you want to keep fairies away, according to folklore, keep a four-leaf clover in your pocket or wear your clothes inside out to ward them off. Like humans, fairies like to have a good time and enjoy parties, banquets, and drinking. Fairy forts are said to be where they carried out their celebrations, and you could travel to their world if they invited you into one—they could even transport you to other parts of the world. However, you had to be careful, given that time doesn't always work the same way there; you could use up years of your life! It is said that the only way to rescue someone from a fairy fort was to pull them out with a branch of a mountain ash tree. But be careful if you reject their invitation: You could be overrun by fairies and unable to get them out of your house and life.

Fairies inhibit standing stones, ancient ringforts, and lone hawthorn trees known as "fairy trees." These sacred places must not be disturbed, or one will face the wrath of the fairies. Once, a farmer plowed over a fairy fort and his farm then experienced crop failure, livestock deaths, and additional bad luck. This superstition remains so powerful that road-building projects in Ireland have been rerouted to avoid disturbing a suspected fairy tree or fort. To ward off fairies and offer protection, Irish folklore developed a rich tradition of charms and rituals to confuse the fairies, using materials they dislike or appealing to a higher power.

Did you know? Leprechauns are Irish fairies!

Leprechauns are considered a particular form of fairy in Irish mythology and folklore. Like other fairies in folklore, leprechauns are described as having magical abilities, though they are distinctly male, solitary, and often cranky or difficult. They are usually depicted as little, red-bearded men, wearing a coat and hat; another consistent trait is their profession as shoemakers, often making shoes for other fairies.

Leprechauns are associated with hidden wealth; their pot of gold is fiercely guarded. AND they are cunning tricksters, known for playing pranks and being tricky to anyone they encounter. If you catch a leprechaun, he may promise to lead you to his hidden pot of gold. However, if you take your eyes off him for even a moment, he will vanish, leaving you empty-handed. In some tales, a captured leprechaun must grant three wishes in exchange for his freedom; however, they are adept at tricking their captors, often twisting wishes to their own advantage. Leprechaun tales show that one should make their own wealth through hard work; it is a waste of time to look for the pot of gold at the end of the rainbow.

Blarney Castle

Ireland has over 30,000 castles and castle ruins. This high number reflects the vital role of controlling land and asserting power throughout Irish history. Castles were defensive strongholds during periods of conflict as well as residences for wealthy families and Gaelic chiefs.

More than 450,000 people visit Blarney Castle and Gardens each year. Located in County Cork, it is not the oldest or largest castle in Ireland, yet it is one the most popular tourist destinations. The castle was built in the medieval tower house style in 1446 by Cormac MacCarthy, a chieftain of Munster.

The most notable aspect of Blarney Castle is the opportunity to kiss The Stone of Eloquence or Blarney Stone, a block of limestone said to give the gift of eloquent speech ("the gift of gab") to those who kiss it.

This stone is located at the top of the castle tower; 128 narrow, steep winding stone steps must be climbed to reach it. The small and narrow width of the stairs was a clever defense feature to limit access to unwanted guests, making the climb claustrophobic and challenging at times. Other forms of castle defensive features include the "murder room" located above the main entrance; this room had a square hole in the floor through which guards could drop rocks and hot oil down onto intruders. In addition, a trap door covering an oubliette, a 15-foot (4.6 meter)-deep stone pit, could be opened to drop unsuspecting intruders into. If you survived the traps and were captured, a hidden network of subterranean tunnels connects to the dungeons.

The Blarney Stone is built into the castle's battlement wall 85 feet (26 meters) above the ground. Once climbers reach the top of the tower, they must hang upside down over this drop to kiss the stone.

It's not for the faint of heart, but is much safer now after the installation of two iron bars to grasp for support. Before the bars were in place, to kiss the stone, a person was held by their ankles and hung upside down off the side of the tower. The stone is occasionally wiped with a cleaner between smooches.

Myths and legends surround the castle and Blarney Stone; there are many versions of the origin of the stone. Common lore says that the goddess Cliodhna enchanted the stone with her magical powers and instructed that it be kissed for good luck. Many believe the stone was gifted in 1314 to Cormac McCarthy as a thank you from King Robert the Bruce from Scotland for providing 4,000 men to defeat the English at the Battle of Bannockburn. McCarthy was the first to kiss the stone, believed it was lucky and incorporated it into the castle's battlements. In 2014, scientists took molecular samples that prove the stone was sourced from a 330-million-year-old limestone that was native to Ireland.

Today, visiting Blarney Castle and the surrounding gardens has much to offer beyond securing the gift of gab. The beautiful, diverse 60-acre landscape gardens feature a beautiful fern garden, woodlands with bamboo, and a rose pergola. The Blarney Castle Poison Garden features plants such as deadly nightshade, castor bean, opium poppy, wolfsbane, mandrake, angel's trumpet, and poison hemlock. The garden's purpose is to educate visitors about poisonous plants, their historical uses, and their dangers, with warnings not to touch, smell, or ingest any plants.

Also on the property is the Rock Close, a mystical place, said to be the site of an ancient druidic settlement. Shaded by a leafy canopy of ancient yew trees, this part of the garden has a feeling of magic. Rocks stand today as they have stood for over 2,000 years. In this mysterious and hidden landscape are a druidic sacrificial altar, a hermit's cell, and a witch's kitchen. Yes, the Blarney Witch has been seen stealing firewood to warm her cave at night for a very long time. Lore says that if you perform the ritual of walking the stones of the witch's staircase, the "wishing steps," backwards with your eyes closed while thinking only of your wish, it will be granted within the year.

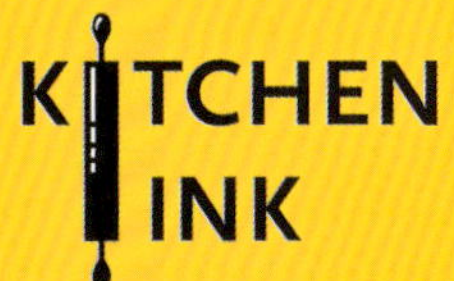

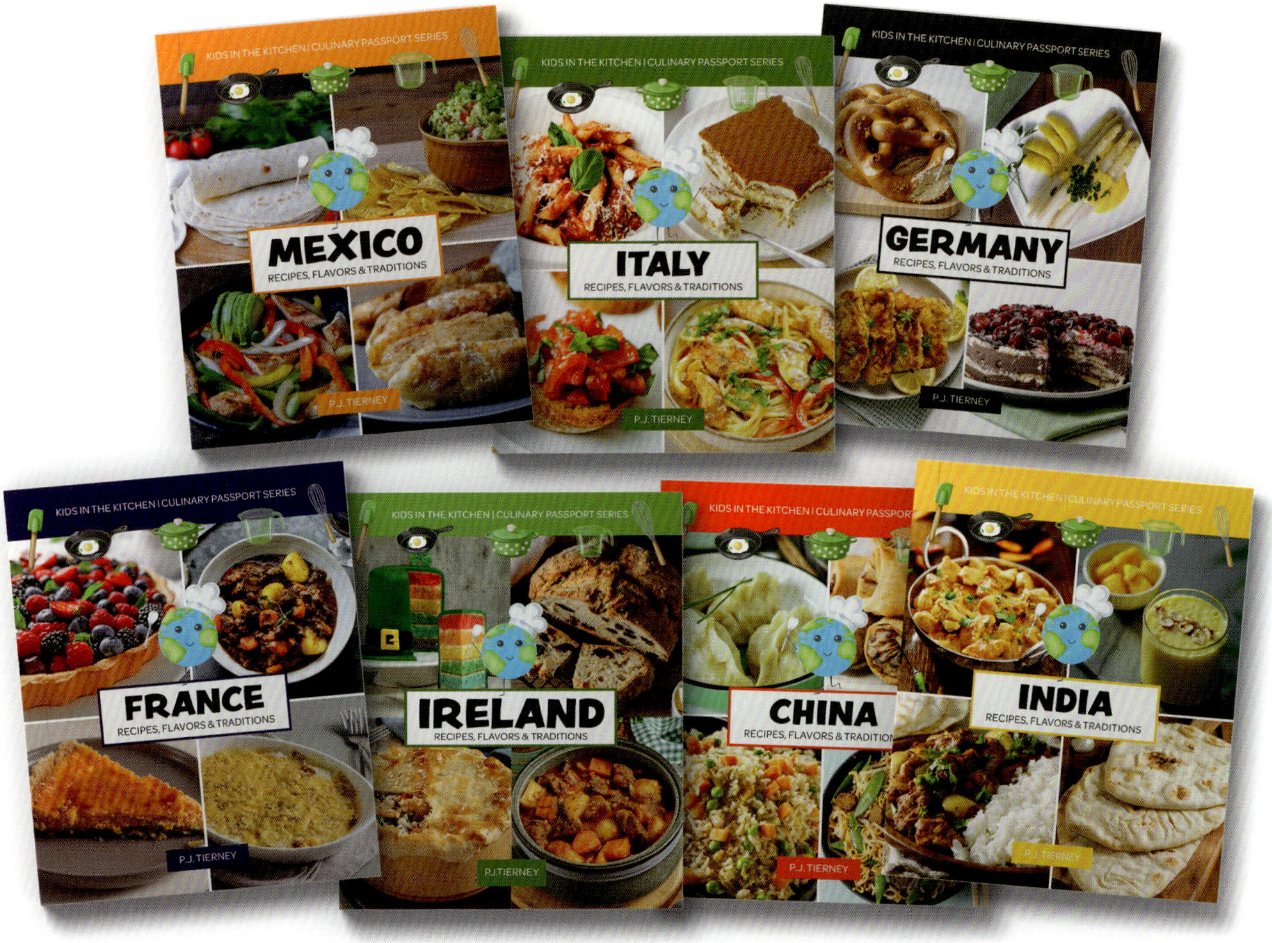

Culinary Passport Series

Discover recipes from all over the world!

Travel around the world from your kitchen.

Where do you want to

travel next?